CRABTREE CONTACT

TOP 10 TALLEST

Ruth Owen

Falls, South America

🌳 Crabtree Publishing Company

www.crabtreebooks.com

Crabtree Publishing Company

www.crabtreebooks.com   1-800-387-7650

PMB 59051   616 Welland Avenue,
350 Fifth Avenue, 59th Floor   St. Catharines, Ontario
New York, NY, 10118   L2M 5V6

Content development by   Published by
Shakespeare Squared   Crabtree Publishing
                               Company © 2010
www.ShakespeareSquared.com
                               First published
No part of this publication may in Great Britain in
be reproduced, copied, stored in 2010 by TickTock
a retrieval system or transmitted in Entertainment Ltd.
any form or by any means electronic,
mechanical, photocopying, recording Printed in the
or otherwise without prior written U.S.A./122009
permission of the copyright owner. CG20091120

Crabtree Publishing
Company credits:
Project manager: Kathy Middleton
Editor: Reagan Miller
Production coordinator: Katherine Berti
Prepress technician: Katherine Berti

TickTock credits:
Publisher: Melissa Fairley
Art director: Faith Booker
Editor: Victoria Garrard
Designer: Emma Randall
Production controller: Ed Green
Production manager: Suzy Kelly

Thank you to Lorraine Petersen and the members of nasen

Picture credits (t=top; b=bottom; c=centre; l=left; r=right; OFC=outside front
cover): Bethel Area Chamber of Commerce: 16–17, 28bl. Bettmann/Corbis:
4. Bryan Berg, Cardstacker: 26, 27, 28tr. Carol Savage Photography: OFC.
Courtesy of Six Flags Great Adventure: 8, 9, 29tl. Ken Fisher/Getty Images: 21.
Getty Images: 6–7, 28tl. iStock: 1, 5 both, 19bl, 20, 22bA, 23bB, 24, 25, 29cr,
29bl. National Geographic/Getty Images: 15. Shutterstock: 2, 10b, 10–11, 12–13,
14–15, 18, 19br, 22bB, 22bC, 22bD, 22bE, 23bA, 23bC, 23bD, 23bE, 28br,
29tr, 29cl, 29br, 31. Steve Sillett: 19t.

Every effort has been made to trace copyright holders, and we apologize in advance
for any omissions. We would be pleased to insert the appropriate acknowledgments
in any subsequent edition of this publication.

Library and Archives Canada Cataloguing in Publication

Owen, Ruth, 1967-
    Top 10 tallest / Ruth Owen.

(Crabtree contact)
Includes index.
ISBN 978-0-7787-7492-1 (bound).--ISBN 978-0-7787-7513-3 (pbk.)

                1. Size perception--Juvenile literature. I. Title.
II. Title: Top ten tallest. III. Series: Crabtree contact

BF299.S5O94 2010   j153.7'52   C2009-906468-5

Library of Congress Cataloging-in-Publication Data

Owen, Ruth, 1967-
   Top 10 tallest / Ruth Owen.
       p. cm. -- (Crabtree contact)
   Includes index.
   ISBN 978-0-7787-7492-1 (reinforced lib. bdg. : alk. paper) --
ISBN 978-0-7787-7513-3 (pbk. : alk. paper)
   1. Size perception--Juvenile literature. I. Title. II. Title: Top ten
tallest. III. Series.

   BF299.S5O94 2010
   152.14'2--dc22

                                                    2009044261

CONTENTS

Mount Everest, Asia

INTRODUCTION

This book is all about the world's tallest things.

From tall people...
...to tall buildings...
...to the tallest mountain on Earth.

Robert Wadlow is the tallest person in recorded history. He was 8.9 feet (2.72 meters) tall.

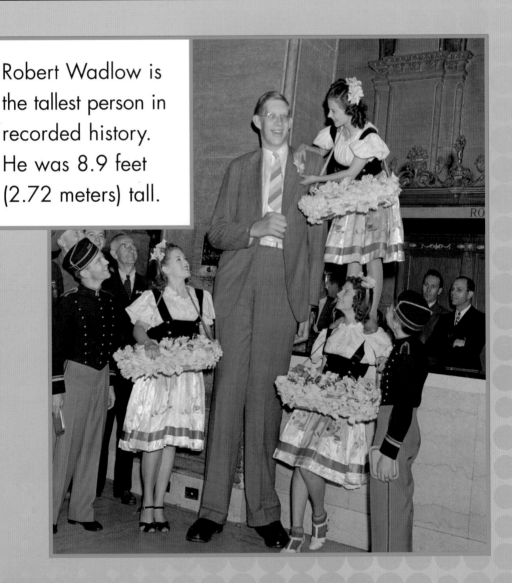

The Burj Dubai in the United Arab Emirates is 0.6 miles (one kilometer) high!

Climbing Mount Everest can be very dangerous. Between 1921 and 2006 the mountain claimed a total of 212 lives.

TALLEST MAN

According to Guinness World Records™,
the world's tallest living man is
named Sultan Kosen.

Sultan is 8.087 feet
(2.465 meters) tall.

Sultan's hands
measure 10.8 inches
(27.5 centimeters).

Sultan lives in Turkey. Guinness World Records™ named him the record holder in 2009. He has visited London and New York to appear on TV.

"The most difficult things are I can't fit into a normal car. I can't go shopping like normal people. I have to have things made specially. The good thing about being so tall is at home they use my height to change the light bulbs and hang the curtains, things like that."
Sultan Kosen

Sultan's feet measure 14.37 inches (36.5 centimeters).

TALLEST ROLLER COASTER

The riders count down...

five, four, three, two, one!

Kingda Ka is 456 feet (139 meters) tall.

You zoom from 0 to 128 miles per hour (206 kilometers per hour) in just 3.5 seconds.

You climb up and up until you are 45 **stories** high!

Then you drop down and down.

It is 59 seconds of terror.

It is Kingda Ka—the world's tallest roller coaster.

Kingda Ka is in New Jersey.

TALLEST BRIDGE

The Millau Viaduct in France is the world's tallest bridge.

The top of the mast on its tallest pylon is 1,125 feet (343 meters) high. That is taller than the Eiffel Tower in Paris, France!

1,062 feet (324 meters)

1,125 feet (343 meters)

Eiffel Tower

Millau Viaduct pylon and mast

Millions of cars drive over the bridge every year. This puts a lot of stress on the bridge. There are **sensors** on the bridge to measure the **stress**.

P2 is the tallest pylon. It is 803.8 feet (245 meters) high.

mast

pylon

TALLEST ICEBERG

An iceberg is a giant chunk of floating ice.

The tallest iceberg ever recorded was spotted in the Atlantic Ocean.

The iceberg measured 551 feet (168 meters). That is the height of a really tall **skyscraper**!

551 feet
(168 meters)

That was its height above **sea level**. However, most of an iceberg is under the water.

No one knows how big the whole iceberg really was!

sea level

13

TALLEST MOUNTAIN

The tallest mountain in the world is Mount Everest. It is in Asia.

Mount Everest is 29,028 feet (8,850 meters) high. The height of a mountain is measured from sea level to its **summit**.

summit

Mount Everest

To reach the summit, climbers must enter the "Death Zone." This is the part of a mountain above 22,965 feet (7,000 meters). There is not a lot of **oxygen** at this height.

Lack of oxygen can make climbers ill. Sometimes they can even die. Most climbers breathe oxygen from tanks.

oxygen mask

oxygen tank

TALLEST SNOWWOMAN

For nine years, the world's tallest snowman was "Angus, King of the Mountain."

Angus was built by the people of Bethel, in Maine. He was 113.5 feet (34.6 meters) tall.

Then, in 2008, Angus lost his record!

The people of Bethel built a new giant—Olympia SnowWoman!

She was 122 feet (37.2 meters) tall. It took over 100 people to build the record-breaking snowwoman.

They used close to 128 million pounds (58 million kilograms) of snow.

tree arms

Olympia SnowWoman

eyelashes made from skis

tires (for her mouth and buttons)

TALLEST TREE

The tallest tree on Earth is a sequoia, or redwood tree. It is found in California.

redwood tree

Scientists think the tree could be 800 years old. It was found by a scientist named Steve Sillett. Steve climbs the world's tallest trees. He studies the trees and measures them.

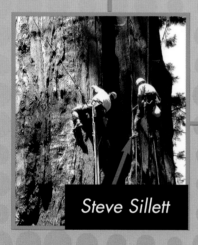

Steve Sillett

Steve climbed to the top of the tallest tree. He dropped a tape measure from the top of the tree down to the ground. It measured 378.9 feet (115.5 meters)!

redwood tree 378.9 feet (115.5 meters)

Statue of Liberty 305 feet (93 meters)

TALLEST WATERFALL

The tallest waterfall in the world is Angel Falls. It is in Venezuela in South America. Angel Falls is 3,211 feet (979 meters) high.

Angel Falls

Some people like to get a really close-up look at the waterfall. They **BASE jump** from the top of Angel Falls!

A BASE jumper jumps from a fixed object. The jumper **freefalls** for a few seconds before opening a parachute.

BASE jumper in freefall

TOP TEN TALLEST HUMAN-BUILT STRUCTURES

Here are the top ten tallest structures in the world. How much taller can we go?

Greenland Square Zifeng Tower
Nanjing, China
1,476 feet
(450 meters)

John Hancock Center
Chicago, USA
1,499 feet
(457 meters)

Shanghai World Financial Center
Shanghai, China
1,614 feet
(492 meters)

Petronas Towers 1 and 2
Kuala Lumpur, Malaysia
1,482 feet (452 meters)

Oriental Pearl Tower
Shanghai, China
1,535 feet
(468 meters)

Taipei 101
Taipei, Taiwan
1,666 feet
(508 meters)

Ostankino Tower
Moscow, Russia
1,771 feet
(540 meters)

Burj Dubai
Dubai, United
Arab Emirates
2,683 feet
(818 meters)

Willis Tower
Chicago, USA
1,729 feet
(527 meters)

CN Tower
Toronto,
Canada
1,814 feet
(553 meters)

TALLEST HUMAN-BUILT STRUCTURE

The Burj Dubai is the world's tallest building and human-built **structure. It is 2,683 feet (818 meters) tall.**

The Burj Dubai

The Burj Dubai is in the United Arab Emirates. The word "burj" means tower in **Arabic**.

Inside the tower there are offices and apartments. There is an outdoor swimming pool on the 78th floor. There is also a hotel designed by fashion designer Georgio Armani.

The tower's elevators have to travel quickly!

The fastest elevator travels at around 33 feet per second (10 meters per second).

TALLEST HOUSE OF CARDS

Bryan Berg is a record-breaking card stacker. In 2007, Bryan built the world's tallest house of cards.

The building is 25.7 feet (7.85 meters) high.
Bryan used 57,240 cards to complete the structure.

Bryan does not use glue or tape.
His secret is to stack the cards in grids.
This makes the buildings strong.

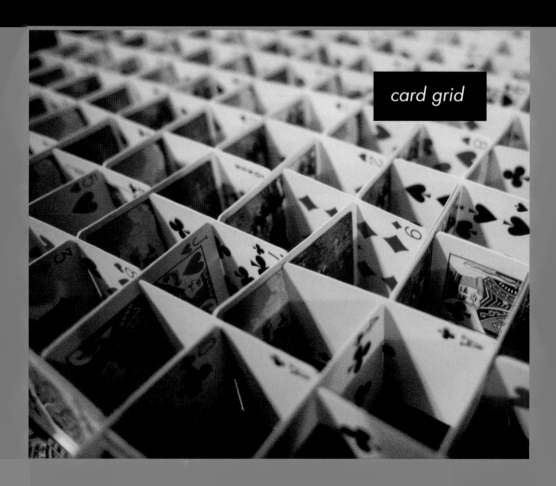

card grid

Bryan Berg and
his house of cards

TOP TEN TALLEST

Some of the tallest things on Earth were created by nature.

Others were built by humans. They are all amazing record breakers.

10

Tallest man:
Sultan Kosen

8.087 feet
(2.465 meters)

9

Tallest House of Cards:
Bryan Berg's
house of cards

25.7 feet (7.85 meters)

8

Tallest Snowwoman:
Olympia SnowWoman

122 feet
(37.2 meters)

7

Tallest tree:
Redwood in California

378.9 feet
(115.5 meters)

6

Tallest roller coaster:
Kingda Ka

456 feet
(139 meters)

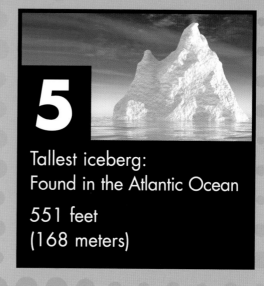

5

Tallest iceberg:
Found in the Atlantic Ocean

551 feet
(168 meters)

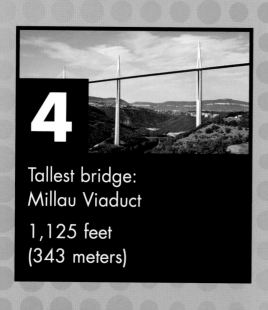

4

Tallest bridge:
Millau Viaduct

1,125 feet
(343 meters)

3

Tallest building:
Burj Dubai

2,683 feet
(818 meters)

2

Tallest waterfall:
Angel Falls

3,211 feet
(979 meters)

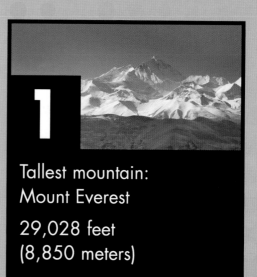

1

Tallest mountain:
Mount Everest

29,028 feet
(8,850 meters)

NEED-TO-KNOW WORDS

Arabic A language spoken in countries such as the United Arab Emirates, Egypt, and Iraq

BASE jump A parachute jump made from a fixed object, such as a high building, instead of from a plane

freefall In skydiving, this is the part of the jump before the parachute opens

Guinness World Records™ An organization that records and measures record-breaking things and events. The world records are then published in a book each year

human-built Created or constructed by humans

oxygen A gas that humans, animals, and plants need in order to live

sea level The surface of the sea. It is used as a starting point for measuring the height of land and mountains

sensor A piece of equipment that can sense things such as movement, sound, heat, light, or pressure

skyscraper A very tall building that tends to dominate a skyline

story One level, or floor, in a building

stress When talking about structures, this word means the forces and pressure on a structure which may cause it to wear away or break

structure Something that has been constructed such as a building, tower, statue, or bridge

summit The highest point, or top, of something

TALL FACTS

platform

cliff

- Mauna Kea is an inactive volcano. It forms part of the iisland of Hawaii. Mauna Keais just over 33,464 feet (10,200 meters) tall. Why is it not the tallest mountain on Earth? That is because mountains are measured from sea level. Only the top 13,795 feet (4,205 meters) of Mauna Kea are above sea level.

- The Royal Gorge Bridge in Colorado, USA, is suspended, or hung, between two giant cliffs. This means it is not a tall bridge, but it is the world's highest bridge. From the platform to the river belowis a drop of 1,053 feet (321 meters).

FIND OUT MORE ONLINE

Find out more facts and figures about the world's tallest skyscraper.
www.burjdubaiskyscraper.com

See pictures and learn more about the world's tallest snowwoman.
www.bethelmainesnowwoman.com/index.html

Learn more about the building of the world's tallest bridge.
www.leviaducdemillau.com/english/divers/gallerie.html

Learn more about Guinness World Records™.
www.guinnessworldrecords.com

Publisher's note to educators and parents:
Our editors have carefully reviewed these Web sites to ensure that they are suitable for children. Many Web sites change frequently, however, and we cannot guarantee that a site's future contents will continue to meet our high standards of quality and educational value. Be advised that children should be closely supervised whenever they access the Internet.

INDEX